"In this unusual and exceptionally interesting work, James Thornton speaks as both a poet who has colonized science and a scientist who speaks a poetic tongue."

EDWARD O. WILSON

"A brilliant introduction to the endless wonders of our universe, from quantum levels to the cosmos. It opened my eyes to many marvels and oddities."

EBERHARD FETZ
Professor of Physiology & Biophysics, University of Washington

"Poets sometimes flinch at the idea of footnotes. Poems, they think, should be perfect small worlds of their own. The Feynman Challenge upends this aesthetic. Like the Pompidou Centre, it wears all its workings on the outside. Plunging into the sea of scientific knowledge, it comes up grinning and glittering with droplets of lovely information. This is a generous book, happy to serve the curiosity, the wonder and humility of science, happening here and there in words that simply send a shudder – *Two black holes are about / to marry, a billion years ago* – through our sense of time and space."

PHILIP GROSS
winner of the T.S.Eliot Prize

JAMES THORNTON is a poet, Zen Buddhist priest, and founder and president of ClientEarth, the leading global not-for-profit law group. As a lawyer, with the Earth as his client, James sees that 'Nature speaks in the grammar of science'. He is a Conservation Fellow of the Royal Zoological Society. The New Statesman named him one of 10 people who could change the world. Irish-American, born in New York, James is also the author of *Client Earth* (Scribe 2018), co-authored with his husband Martin Goodman, which received the Judges' Selection, Business Book of the Year Award 2018, and the Green Prize for Sustainable Literature from Santa Monica Public Library. He has twice won Leader of the Year at the Business Green Awards. For his legal work, The Financial Times awarded him its Lifetime Achievement Award. His writing includes two novels, a book of spiritual practice, and three volumes of poetry. He was a judge for the 2020 Laurel Awards for Ecopoetry. He lives in Los Angeles and London.

The Feynman Challenge

JAMES THORNTON

BARBICAN PRESS

For Martin

Acknowledgements

This collection was edited by Nigel McLoughlin, poet, Professor of Creativity & Poetics at the University of Gloucestershire, and editor of the literary journal *Iota*. He also brings a scientist's eye, with a master's degree in neuropsychology. My text has benefited from his attention.

I have worked to get the science right. Five senior scientists have helped vet the science.

They are: Howard Covington, physicist and mathematician, Chair of the Alan Turing Institute; Eberhard Fetz, Professor of Physiology & Biophysics, University of Washington; Richard Fortey, palaeontologist, formerly of the Natural History Museum in London; Peter Landrock, cryptographer and mathematician, member of Microsoft's Technical Advisory Board, and founder of Cryptomathic; and Edward O. Wilson, sociobiologist, entomologist, and evolutionary theorist, University Professor Emeritus, Harvard University.

I am indebted to them. Where they found problems I have turned my pencil around and used the eraser. I own any remaining errors.

Finally thanks to Martin Goodman and Peter Thornton, whose readings and suggestions pushed me back to the page.

Contents

Look at the stars! look, look up at the skies!

GERARD MANLEY HOPKINS
THE STARLIGHT NIGHT

Our culture is foolish to keep science and poetry separated: they are two tools to open our eyes to the complexity and beauty of the world.

CARLO ROVELLI
REALITY IS NOT WHAT IT SEEMS:
THE JOURNEY TO QUANTUM GRAVITY

Introduction

Poets say science takes away from the beauty of the stars—mere globs of gas atoms. I too can see the stars on a desert night, and feel them. But do I see less or more? The vastness of the heavens stretches my imagination—stuck on this carousel my little eye can catch one-million-year-old light. A vast pattern—of which I am a part... What is the pattern, or the meaning, or the why? It does not do harm to the mystery to know a little about it. For far more marvelous is the truth than any artists of the past imagined it. Why do the poets of the present not speak of it? What men are poets who can speak of Jupiter if he were a man, but if he is an immense spinning sphere of methane and ammonia must be silent?

RICHARD FEYNMAN[1]

When I first read Feynman's remarks on poetry, I received them as a challenge. "I will write those poems," I said to myself. Thus this collection was born, slowly. What I thought to finish in a year has taken five. Really it all started for me a long time ago.

As a teenager I loved the pre-Socratics, the Greek philosophers who preceded the Athenian contrarian. It is hard not to fall for these thinkers, emerging from the darkness with speculations that seem simulacra of modern theories.

Xenophenes saw seashell fossils on a mountain and deduced that the mountain once lay under the sea. Isn't that wonderful more than 2000 years before Lyell laid down the principles of geology? What are more beguiling than Zeno's paradoxes, which demonstrate that motion is not possible? Perhaps most striking is the atomic theory of Democritus.

Only fragments of Democritus' work remain. This is a shame because he wrote voluminously on philosophy, sense perception, mathematics, and a variety of scientific subjects. But his vision is captured by Lucretius in the great poem *De Rerum Natura*, or On the Nature of Things.

The atomists created what seems a strikingly modern view, given it emerged in 5th Century BC Greece. They denied that supernatural agency has anything to do with the world. Instead, the world emerged out of an original chaos, in which atoms floated free. As the atoms cohered, gradually a world and living things formed. Atoms are irreducible, of many kinds, and their coming together in mixtures produces the different things we experience. Between atoms is void, with more empty space between atoms of air than atoms of iron.

We sense things, say the atomists, when our sense organs encounter atoms. Because our organs differ somewhat between people, and greatly between people and animals, people perceive the same objects or events differently, and people and animals greatly so. Only reason, operating on the data of the senses, can perceive cause and effect, which rule how atoms combine and all things occur.

The atomists had what looks like an early theory of evolution too. Living things spontaneously adapt to changing circumstances, and people changed from an early pre-linguistic form into us by banding together into tribal units and learning new behaviours.

Democritus opened a new world. It must have felt wonderful to do this work. Four centuries on, Lucretius immortalized it. *De Rerum Natura* is his only surviving poem and we are lucky to have it. Lucretius has always been in the pantheon of poets, praised in antiquity by Cicero, Ovid and Quintillian. Montaigne, in his essay *Of Books,* says Lucretius is one of the four poets who "hold the first rank by very far."[2]

Lucretius' poem is of epic length. Two modern editions come in at around 300 pages, and it sells well compared to modern poets. Lucretius lays out the atomist view with such vividness that his poem had a major impact on the development of science. As a pair of commentators put it:

> [t]he Lucretian conception of nature as 'accomplishing everything by herself spontaneously and independently and free from the jurisdiction of the gods' was a major driving force in the Scientific Revolution experienced in Western Europe beginning in the seventeenth century. Over the following three centuries the theory of atoms was converted from a poetic fantasy to a well-confirmed empirical hypothesis, the clear, consoling power, and provocation of Lucretius' poem contributing in no small measure to this result.[3]

What I love in Democritus is the freedom, the originality, the genius of hitting on the atomic theory by intuition and *Gedankenexperimenten,* by geometry and reason. This kind of thinking reminds me of the way that modern greats like Einstein worked. Democritus did not have a large audience in the Athens of his day, but he could hardly have wished for a better evangelist than Lucretius to speak to the audience of history.

Nor was Lucretius' work evangelism only. He creates a sweeping account of mind and consciousness, of matter and the meaning of life, or perhaps the lack of it. In the poem, the atomic theory is linked to a satisfyingly complete vision of what it means to be a conscious organism alive in the physical world.

So poetry about science, at least science when it still took the form of natural philosophy, is no new thing. It was central to the Western canon. But it has become less so over time, as science has become more central and powerful, more complex and, as many see it, more threatening.

Mary Midgley, in her indispensable *Science and Poetry*,[4] argues that science and scientists were praised down through the Enlightenment, as in Pope's famous lines on Newton.[5] By the time of the Romantics, distrust of science had grown, through a reasonable dislike of the industrialization it allowed. This aversion was expressed in the poetry, perhaps most memorably in Blake's image of Satanic mills.

Midgley points to Wordsworth nevertheless seeing that the day might come when it was possible to write poetry on science. He writes:

> The remotest discoveries of the Chemist, the Botanist or Mineralogist will be the proper objects of the Poet's art as any on which it can be employed, *if the time should ever come when these things shall be familiar to us...manifestly and palpably material to us as enjoying and suffering beings.*[6]

Midgley then goes on to ask what kind of poet could write that kind of poetry. She says:

> The kind of author who would be needed to write this kind of poetry would, then, have to be someone for whom the details of a science are *as familiar and as palpably material* as the topics with which poetry normally deals—topics which are mainly concerned with central human emotions and with the world as we directly perceive it.[7]

She continues to ask the vital question for us:

> Could anyone who was not himself a scientist possibly stand in this relation to the highly technical 'remotest discoveries' of modern science? It is surely not easy to see how Wordsworth's gifted outsiders, eager to follow in the steps of the man of science, could ever reach this kind of familiarity with the details of the subject.[8]

The 'gifted outsider' may be so rare, or not exist at all, she offers, that we may need to wait till scientists become interested in writing poetry to get poems that proceed from an understanding of the science.

In distinction to the hard road facing the 'gifted outsider', she posits another path. This is for the poet who does not aspire to take the reader to the heart of the science, but who writes about

[t]he 'general indirect effects' of the sciences—the interface between them and ordinary life—[which] is a topic available to all of us.[9]

This second kind of poetry about science, then, which considers how science interacts with ordinary life, is an open road for any poet to travel, in her view.

Midgley's dichotomy is salutary. She has in effect produced a taxonomist's cladogram, splitting the species of poets who write about science. The first is the non-scientist outsider trying to write about science from the inside. The second is the ordinary person's perspective of how science impacts life.

There is a contemporary world of poets inspired by science. Some are writing about the impacts of science on life. Others though, more perhaps than Midgley would have thought, aim to write from the heart of science. They are paying attention to how scientists think, to how graphene folds, to gene manipulation, animal migration and the origin of stars. They know there is no end of wonder when you follow the science, and they need to express it.

Let me declare my loyalties as a poet when it comes to science. My own work is that of the outsider trying to write from the heart of science. This is the path Feynman challenges us to take.

While not a scientist I am happy in their company. My first great mentor was the entomologist Alice Gray at the American Museum of Natural History in New York, and I may have become a biologist under her influence, had the environmental movement not started. Its core realization of the need for a societal *volte face* in our dealings with the rest of nature led me to put aside the biology and philosophy studies I loved (I often recall with pleasure the graduate course in the evolutionary biology of arthropods I was allowed to take while a philosophy undergrad at Yale) to move to law so that I could protect the natural world.

Environmental law often means working with scientists, and the evolution of law in this field to keep pace with emerging science is its most interesting aspect. Most recently I've been proud to be an author on pieces in *Nature*.

For a number of years between episodes of practising environmental law, I enjoyed running a neuroscience research institute. One of my fondest memories there is from a day when some of my scientists and I met with a senior scientist representing the foundation we were trying to raise research funds from. We had a multi-hour meeting in which I described our proposed research in detail and showed why it was both novel and important. When we were done and the scientist on the other side of the table agreed to recommend our proposal, he asked me where I'd gotten my doctorate in neuroscience. When he found out I was an outsider he was surprised, saying that only a neuroscientist should have been able to answer the questions he had put to me.

Fond as I am of his mistake, the truth is that I am an outsider and not a scientist. When I pick up a paper in *Nature,* I am hounded and intrigued by my ignorance. I cannot say with Aquinas that I have understood every page that I have read. What excites me is that science opens unseen pastures, unknown valleys, entire universes of beauty and complexity, of challenge and chaos. It calls us into a future of terror and tranquillity, it offers us the opportunity to study the conflict in our breast and so hope to survive the coming crises.

The coming environmental crises featured prominently in a public conversation that the poet Robert Hass had with the biologist E. O. Wilson around the time I started this collection. The former American Poet Laureate and the Pulitzer Prize winning scientist discuss how the arts and science interact. Hass asks Wilson

"Do you have any recommendation for poets?" Wilson answers, "Colonize science." [10]

It is a good strategy for an outsider to become a colonist. Colonize science is what I do.

Is a work like Lucretius' still possible? Could there be one so mammoth and coherent? Sir Martin Smith, founder of the Oxford Smith School of Enterprise and Environment, when I first mentioned my project to him, suggested that quantum entanglement deserved its own epic the length of the *Iliad*. Perhaps I will be given the time and learn the science to write it. I did, though, make another quantum bargain. Peter Landrock, founder and head of Cryptomathic, told me over lunch that if I was taking up Feynman's challenge, I must do a poem on quantum cryptography. Judge the result for yourself; at least there must not be many poems that colonize the topic.

It is not possible in a poem, even one as long as Lucretius', to convey the full domain of modern theory and its relation to life as he did. This is no cause for alarm. As consumers of contemporary writing we are used to accepting parts rather than wholes, dioramas rather than worlds, viewing points rather than atlases. Writing about the partial imposes a kind of humility. If we remember it is partial, a pull to wholeness also emerges. If I have a unifying theme it is thrill and gratitude for life and mind and the threat we offer these in the Anthropocene.

Below the surface of scientific language lies poetry. My ear bends close to scientists' discourse, to pick out their diction of discovery. A few lines in a paper in *Nature* can consume hours and compel many drafts until my words are consonant with the source and achieve poetry. To enter the material, connect it with the beat of our human heart, and deliver a text with clarity beyond the reach of prose, is the aim.

The attitude we take is central. How do we approach the material, the world? Do we start in the stark honesty of our ignorance, that most hopeful of places, then study passionately till what we study speaks through us unfeigned and unadulterated? Are we refashioned in the encounter as much as we fashion the material? Are we surprised by where the study takes us, where the science points? Do we go there whether we want to or not? Are we surprised by the language that comes out of us; do we then polish it through the years and hours and a Dylan Thomas number of drafts?

Science and poetry approach the Real in piety. Lucretius tells us that 'true piety lies...in the power to contemplate the universe with a quiet mind.' [11]

This quiet mind was known to Feynman and to Einstein. It is known today to all creative scientists and artists. This mind is the source of the wonder Feynman points to. My poems attempt to share this place of wonder. Some of them try to add something to the science, something that was in Lucretius and Democritus but is generally missing in the way we do science now. These poems consider a moral dimension. The moral dimension arises either as a result of a use of science that has harmed the natural world, as in the poems 'Spat' and 'The rules of loss', or because the science provides new perspectives on who we are, as in 'A bulletin from our branch' and 'The conquest of Earth'.

To touch the inside of the science and add a moral dimension makes a poem into a dojo we can enter to fight out some of the most complex dilemmas we face. Go ahead. While some of these poems are meant to induce wonder gently, others are meant to start a fight.

When I go into a fight I may win or lose but I like to line up my forces. So not only have I studied in my outsider way, and tried to colonize the science, I have lined up scientists to correct the error of my ways. Inevitably and despite all their efforts much of the mud of my errors will remain stuck.

There are several sources for these poems. Some derive from old preoccupations, like 'Too few to fill the sky', 'Aerial wars' and

'Tomb blossoms'. Some from new discoveries that happened during the years it took to write the poems, like 'Traumatic matings', 'Fringed with teeth' and 'A map of peculiar velocities'. Some grow from my lifelong empathy with the natural world, and pain from our maiming it, such as 'Chiropterans', 'Count those lost' and 'Coelacanths among us'.

In writing the poems, I have tried to make the science 'familiar and palpably material'. I offer footnotes so that knowing the source material, you can see how it is reflected in the work, and also find further reading.

Our emotions are new in every generation, so they will be central to poetry as long as it is practised. Feynman is right to add that science brings new pages to this traditional tablet. The openings of science will never stop. The opportunity they offer for creative expression is boundless. In Zen we talk about enlightenment experiences as openings. New scientific discoveries are openings in this way too. Let us contemplate them with the quiet mind of Lucretius and work hard on our poems.

LONDON AND PÉZILLA DE CONFLENT

NOTES

1 Feynman, R.P., *et al., The Feynman Lectures on Physics* (New York: Basic Books, 50th anniv. ed. 2011), fn 3–11.

2 Montaigne, M., *The Complete Works* (London: Everyman's Library 2003), 362. The other three in Montaigne's personal pantheon are Virgil, Catullus and Horace.

3 Johnson, M., & Wilson, C., *The Cambridge Companion to Lucretius* (Cambridge: University of Cambridge Press 2007), 147.

4 Midgley, M., *Science and Poetry* (Abingdon: Routledge Classics 2006).

5 'Nature and Nature's laws lay hid in night / God said, "let Newton be!" and there was light.' The lines are from Pope's epitaph for Newton, *quoted in* Midgley, *supra* at 64.

6 Preface to the Second Edition of the Lyrical Ballads, *Wordsworth's Poetical Works,* ed. Thomas Hutchinson (Oxford: Oxford University Press 1936), 939, *quoted in* Midgley *supra* at 76 with emphasis added.

7 Midgley, *supra* at 76.

8 Id. Scientists themselves live the inner relation with science and some are wonderful poets, like Rebecca Elson, *see A Responsibility to Awe* (Oxford: OxfordPoets 2001).

9 Id., 77.

10 Wilson, E.O., & Hass, R., *The Poetic Species* (New York: Bellevue Literary Press 2014), 77.

11 Lucretius, *On the Nature of Things,* Book V, Lines 1200–1203, *quoted in* Midgley *supra* at 32.

CENSUS OF DEEP LIFE

Two klicks down in solid rock it teems
with life. Bacteria are everywhere.
A group of nineteen kinds are found
down gold mines in South Africa,
in methane pockets under ocean floor off
Indonesia, under Alaska, Canada,
Italy, Scandinavia, everywhere we look.

It's unlike that on the surface:
where are the orang-utans of Montreal
or the polar bears of Sumatra?
Yes, you will say, but the weather
at the poles is cooler than the equator
while comfortably similar deep down.

Species cross the globe in ways we
can imagine doing. Birds wing their way
while spiders balloon on parachutes
of silk and many seeds hitch rides.
Yet how did this small kith of depth
microbes move planet wide through rock?

Developing clues favour serpentines,
laid down some four billion years ago
around the time of life's beginning.

They could have evolved just once
when all the land on Earth was one
then spread apart through the slow
ballet of tectonic plates.

                    While daily
crises fill our short attention span
the bacteria miles below our feet
keep thriving in their measured
metabolic way.
                    When the Sun in its
cycle of birth and death swells out,
parching then sterilizing the planetary
surface we call home, it is likely
they will be there, dependable.
Living the ultimate *vie cachée,* this
group of bugs is invested in futures.

Brohic, C., Deep Earth zombie bugs went global, *New Scientist* (14 Dec 2013), 12.

Embodied semantics

When we read a novel our brain
changes. Our language regions
light up, but here is the surprise:
our sensory motor areas, the parts
that let us dance and play the violin,
run shadow activity and build more
connections. The changes last
days after we put the book down.

Our brain behaves like we inhabited
the characters and remember their
movements. You were them says brain.
You were Anna Karenina, you became
Proust and Maigret, Socrates and Gollum.
You are them, long after you close them
in their book and shelve it.

Does watching a film give the brain
the same full body experience?
You don't build and inhabit a world
as a watcher like you do as a reader
so I doubt it.
                We'll see if I'm right
when someone does the fMRI scans.
Meanwhile it's back to my thriller, back
to full body learning. Today we're dodging
bullets and roping steers in sagebrush.

Berns, G.S., *et al.,* Short- and Long-Term Effects of a Novel on Connectivity in the Brain, *Brain Connectivity* 3, 590 (9 Oct 2013), doi:10.1089/brain.2013.0166.

OF MICE AND SCORPIONS

Bark scorpions can be deadly
if you come upon them
in the Sonoran desert
where food items are scarce
and they are plentiful.

For the grasshopper mouse, distant
cousin of the house mouse,
scorpion is always on the menu.

A mouse who grabs a scorpion
in its paws gets stung but avoids
agony through clever wiring. Pain
in mammals flows when two sodium
channels work: one initiates
the signal, the other propagates it.

In the grasshopper mouse
the second channel is custom built:
scorpion venom fires the initiating
channel like in any mammal
but blocks the second and so
pain dies away before it is felt.

The difference is down to a single
amino acid in the second channel,
a good molecule to study for pain
relief. Meantime under the Sonoran
sun, little paws hold firm
and scorpion goes down like sushi.

If you're hungry you can often
find them on the underside of things
because bark scorpions climb walls
and trunks and have the habit
of negative geotaxis, preferring
to look at the world from upside down.

Zhang, S., Rodent Immune to Scorpion Venom, *Nature News,*
doi:10.1038/nature.2013.14014.

Rowe, A.H., *et al.,* Voltage-Gated Sodium Channel in Grasshopper Mice
Defends Against Bark Scorpion Toxin, *Science* 342, 441–446 (25 Oct
2013), doi:10.1126/science.1236451.

Rumination and forest bathing

Rumination is good for cows
but in us signifies, when psychologists
use the word, the repetitive grinding
turn of thought, the inner Catherine wheel
of obtrusive ideation, the sharp blades
of negativity the mind is stretched across
and attention cannot turn from.

Until you take a walk in nature.
Our animal has evolved with the rest
of life. Our thoughts, our feelings,
our perceptions all arose in the field
and we carry them into cities.

How much time did the hunter gatherer
stare out at the hills, replenishing
his attention, then walk quiet
through polymorphous woods?
How often did his partner
finding the compatibility
feeling the fascination
by study of living signs
feed her family when he
returned home without a kill?

When we became farmers we still bent
to Earth and under sky. Even the priests
and lawmakers we invented
still visited the land, for our urbanity
had narrow compass upon the living globe.

Now half of all of us live in cities
and by mid century three quarters.
While cities create culture and reduce
the global footprint of our proliferating kind,
with the towers mental illness also rises.

An experiment: walk in an urban
area with traffic or in a quiet park.
The two walks play differently in brain.

When the subgenual part
of the prefrontal cortex is active
you feel withdrawal and you ruminate,
the looped negatives not only painful
but a risk factor for mental illness.

The result of the experiment is
simple and powerful: the nature
walk quiets this brain area
while the urban walk does not.

By cutting ourselves from nature
we lose a remedy we evolved
one that cuts the loops of thought
that welcome illness in.

The Japanese take forest baths
by walking in woodland. Our ever
growing cities need space for us
to take forest baths, grassland baths,
garden baths, any way we can
affiliate with the living world and
reset our so ruminating brains.

Bratman, G., *et al.*, Nature experience reduces rumination and subgenual prefrontal cortex activation, *Proceedings of the National Academy of Sciences* 112, 8567–8572 (14 July 2015), doi:10.1073/pnas.1510459112.

Bratman, G., *et al.*, The benefits of nature experience: improved affect and cognition, *Landscape and Urban Planning* 138 (Mar 2015), 41–50, doi:10.1016/j.landurbplan.2015.02.005.

A DOZEN WAYS TO MAKE A LIVING

When life punched up into the third
dimension from the flatness of bacterial
slime it explored a living geometry
of fractal fronds of rods and circular quilts
testing every kind of symmetry at scales
from peppercorn to golf umbrella opened.

You can find their traces everywhere
but Antarctica, and they dominated
the world for a hundred million years
longer than us, if their meditative style
could be said to dominate. Perhaps fill
is closer, they filled the world, quiet
in the deep and shallow seas, some
taking nutrients by osmosis
others hosting green bacteria.

After a century and a half of arguing
we think they had their own genesis
unrelated to modern forms.
Later life did not elaborate
the path they blazed but arose
apart and followed a different course.

Imagine theirs as a peaceable kingdom
without predators or parasites
testing only a dozen of the ninety-two
ways ecologists say that one can make a living.

Animals not plants, mostly sessile, many
of them fronds with holdfasts sensibly
filled with sand, their fossilised remains
first found in the Charnwood Forest and
so called *Charnia*. These grew into elegant
animal forests that swayed in the tides.

Was their primacy ended by fresh forms
born into the Cambrian, with their twenty
new ways to make a living, including predators
mobile and clever, to cull the animal
forests and so feed their novel hunger?

Those fossils hastily composed in sand beds
after ancient storms and more detailed ones
layered in ash are enigmatic on their decline.

And now we may have met them, these Ediacarans.

Trawling through specimens pulled
decades ago from Tasmanian deeps
then fixed in formaldehyde, researchers
found two small creatures shaped
like mushrooms with a simple gut in an elegant
body of jelly and failed to classify them
among the existing families of life.

They look like Ediacarans and lived like
Ediacarans. When we find their living
peers we can test their DNA to see if
they are remote from forms life finds
fashionable now. I suspect they are.

So we may have found surviving Ediacarans
who have quietly pursued their living
for an extra five hundred million years
alongside their more complex successors.

Rincon, P., Deep sea 'mushroom' may be new branch of life, bbc.
in/1qqnX1H (3 Sept 2014), retrieved 2 Feb 2017.

Just, J., *et al., Dendrogramma,* New Genus, with Two New Non-Bilaterian
Species from the Marine Bathyal of Southeastern Australia (Animalia,
Metazoa *incertae sedis*)—with Similarities to Some Medusoids from the
Precambrian Ediacaran, *PlosOne* (3 Sept 2014), doi:10.1371/journal.
pone.0102976.

The future of clouds

When I first saw clouds from the other side
I wanted to open the pressure door leap
down and romp on them unhindered
to find in their billowy lawns and crevasses
an unexampled canvas uncoloured by man.

Later I rode through a sky populated
by gigantic cumulus brains separate
in all directions each flashing internal
lightning as if thinking thoughts too grand
for my species to contain. In unison
they worked and contrapuntally filled dim
heaven with their ungraspable brilliance.

The future of clouds is a serious matter.
Were all clouds to pull a runner and fill
the sky no more then Earth would burn
to cinders so much do they cool us.

In the hierarchy of clouds the most important
are those slung low over tropical seas.

And what will come of them as the planet
warms? Will they work their cooling or be
driven off by the indifference displayed in
our ways like the gods of Greece and Egypt?

There is some good news: warmer air
above could hold low clouds in place.
But there is also bad: water vapour is their
key ingredient, like gin in a G & T, and warmer
air above may wick the clouds away.

The narrative of clouds seems moving
in the direction of ever less cover. So as with
more and more things that force my eyes open
I plan to deepen my appreciation of clouds.

Battersby, S., Clear Skies: Our future is looking less cloudy and that is
far from good, *New Scientist* (6 Sept 2014), 42, doi:10.1016/S0262–
4079(14)61725–5.

Tan, I., *et al.,* Observational constraints on mixed-phase clouds
imply higher climate sensitivity, *Science* 352, 224–227 (8 Apr 2016),
doi:10.1126/science.aad5300.

The jaguar sometimes bites

In the jungle I've heard it said
that when anteater and jaguar meet
the anteater would walk on
but the jaguar sometimes bites
through the anteater's skull
and feasts on its flesh. Other times
the anteater uses its great claws
to rip the jaguar apart then ambles
off to make a meal of termites.

Giant anteater and jaguar are both
rare though widespread. This is the
law of the jungle. Diversity is so high
that the numbers of any living thing
are seldom strong. We enjoy flocks
of birds in the north, a single species
dazzling with its flamingo pink, its
snow goose white, the warm surprise
of seeing so many thrushes at once.

But when, after a time of great quiet,
a flock filters through the jungle, you
see they are not one but dozens
of unrelated kinds. Since each species is
too few to fill a flock, jointly teeming
gives members of unrelated clans
the protection from predators that
makes flocking feel right. Antshrikes
join manikins, screamers, cotingas,

honeycreepers, euphonias, names
whose glamour hints at the marvel
of meeting these creatures fleeting.

Sentinel species give notice when
predators appear. They also have
a sideline in deceit. When a sentinel
is after an insect and another flock
member is after it too, the sentinel
sounds a false alarm. This frights
the flock and so costs the whole
troop but distracts the rival and bags
the sentinel the disputed meal.

A flock lives as one for years together
and builds nests companionably close.
When mixed flocks meet, each species looks
to its own kind in the rival flock and chides
them with song and chatter, telling them
to take a powder, get lost, leave the trees
and all the fodder to my friends and me.

Engulfed in birds you'll see that while
they briefly own a patch by infesting it
they harmonize by diverging.

Some find ants on the floor, some termites
on branches, some take insects from leaves,
others from trunks of trees, some winkle
arthropods from dried leaves in forest litter.

You sense too that powerful moments
in nature are often subtle wonders.
Driving by you'd miss them.

Leading the way when the flock moves quiet
and on its own foraging through shadows
will be a dun, little burnished one of them,
say a bush tanager, so they can enter dim.

Forsyth, A., *Nature of the Rainforest* (Ithaca: Cornell University Press 2008), 37–45 (high biodiversity but low populations of individual species in tropical forests).

Kricher, J., *A Neotropical Companion* (Princeton: Princeton University Press, 2d ed. 1997), 34 (rarity usual in many species in lowland tropics), 39; 251–2; 265 (composition and behaviour of mixed avian flocks).

Symbiont real estate

Corals live a symbiotic life. Animals
and algae meet each other's
needs and build stone villas for fish.

Too much heat makes corals
bleach and die, so when in stress
they work to cool the neighbourhood.

Sulphur compounds bubble to the sky
and convene water droplets into clouds.

Clouds in turn then cool the reef
and maintain its value as real estate.

My own boundaries shift to know
that polyps change the weather.

Raina, J.-B. *et al.,* DSMP biosynthesis by an animal and its role in
coral thermal stress response, *Nature* 502, 677–680 (31 Oct 2013),
doi:10.1038/nature12677.

Páramos

The eternal war between grasses
and trees reached a local truce
in northern Andes when mountains
rose up three miles. Here is a place
trees neither grasp nor reach.

Grasslands flourish and the clock
of plant evolution ticks faster
than anywhere else on Earth.

Sunlight pours down but this high
you're bathed in unwelcome ultraviolet
and it gets bone numbing cold.

One of the marvels here devised is
a tree tall daisy. It tops its petals with
white hairs to fend off radiation and
wraps its trunk in a coat of dead leaves so
vital juices stay just warm enough to flow.

This verse follows Carl Zimmer's article in the *New York Times:* Zimmer, C.,
Fast-Paced Evolution in the Andes, nyti.ms/2kXz2c7, retrieved 2 Feb 2017.

See also Madriñán, S., *et al.,* Páramo is the world's fastest evolving and
coolest biodiversity hotspot, *Frontiers in Genetics* 4: 192 (9 Oct 2013),
doi:10.3389/fgene.2013.00192.

The apex predator guild

Not Utah as we know it now
a desert where Mormons
hoard their wives in Moab,
but the lush wet littoral of the Western
Interior Seaway, separating the east
and west coasts of North America
with shallow Jurassic waters.

Meat eating dinosaurs here achieved
great size. *Siats meekororum,*
genus and species new, is emerging
from rocks laid down ninety-eight
million years ago. *Siats* in his heyday
dominated the apex predator guild.

If you wanted to be boss, he was
tough to challenge: the therapod
version of a billionaire, able
to ignore whom he pleased and
eat whom he wanted, safe in being
the dominating carnivore.

Tyrannosaurus rex had not
yet joined, ineligible
since his genes lay in generations
still just the size of a house pet.

By the Late Cretaceous luck changed
for *Siats*. He went out of business.
T. rex seized the chance to ramp up
to twice the size of the older boss.
He became apex in the guild and ran
it for another twenty million years.

Zanno, L.E., *et al.*, Neovenatorid therapods are apex predators in the Late
Cretaceous of North America, *Nature Communications* 4, article no. 2827
(22 Nov 2013), doi:10.1038/ncomms3827.

Your inner fish

By the 1840s, Earth was yielding up
by the cartload and from many places
fossils of mammal-like reptiles.
We saw in them a transitional series over time
as life took reptiles and made mammals.
But an earlier episode was missing.
Who first crossed the tide line that separates
water from land?
                    In 2006 she appeared
under the pick of palaeontologists
on Canada's Ellesmere Island. She was
a walking fish whose fins became legs
on her descendants. This link to the sea
was named Tiktaalik by Inuit elders
in whose land she slept.

"Big Freshwater Fish" is our ancestor
or else another fish who stepped
from the sea. Faulkner has his idiot
Benjy say, "My mother is a fish." He's
only off in his count of generations.

Before fish we are protists, then
worms whose notochord turns
into our spinal stem so Beethoven
conducts symphonies. After fish
we are reptiles. Their parts live on
in us in three middle ear bones:
hammer, anvil and stirrup.

                                   Stirrup was
the hind bone in our fish jaw. Hammer
and anvil are from our reptile jaws.
Repurposed, hammer strikes anvil
and stirrup carries sound so we
inhabit a nuanced aural world
rich in tonal variance as a coral reef in
forms of life. Fish have no ears
and reptiles primitive ones. Bone
migration lets us hear the world.

How hard was it to step onto land?
Though Tiktaalik deserves an epic,
it may not have been so hard.
Birchir fish, from African fresh waters,
haul themselves ashore. Made to stay
on land eight months, their skeletons
change so walking on fins is easier.

Developmental plasticity induced by
dry land could have boosted traits
our ancestors needed to walk. Our
forebear fish may have morphed
from reptile to mammal more sleekly
than we credit. But then we often take
our forebears a little bit for granted.

Neil Shubin discovered, dug out and understood Tiktaalik. His book about it is compelling: Shubin, N., *Your Inner Fish* (New York: Pantheon 2008), 22–27; 161–64.

Standen, E. M., *et al.,* Developmental plasticity and the origin of tetrapods, *Nature* 513, 54–58 (4 Sept 2014), doi:10.1038/nature13708.

Barras, C., Adapt first, mutate later, *New Scientist* (14 Jan 2015), 26–30.

CRISPR, the new gene editing tool, is helping us see how fish fins turned into tetrapod legs, *see* Callaway, E., CRISPR's hopeful monsters: gene-editing storms evo-devo labs, *Nature News* (17 Aug 2016), doi:10.1038/nature.2016.20449.

Tomb blossoms

Figs multiply prodigiously in warm
regions of the world, where live today
nine hundred kinds of them, in forms diverse
as trees, both evergreen and deciduous,
vines, scandent shrubs, epiphytes, and stranglers.

In all this ramiculation
of the family history of figs, you will never
see a single flower, even if you
climb in the canopy with the hungry
mangabey. Figs are alone in the world
in keeping their flowers inside the fruit.

How then do figs set seed?
With help from wasps, and not just
any wasps. In the great book of evolution
the story of fig and wasp has been inscribed
for over a hundred years. Here's why—
on each kind of fig, a unique wasp makes
its living, small as half a rice grain.

Scents from the hidden blooms perfuse
the ostiole, a tiny hole in the fig's
bottom protected by inturned scales.
A female wasp, newly emerged, intent
and bedecked with pollen from her natal
fruit, flies as much as ten kilometres
over the forest recruiting for a
receptive fig.

It is not easy to enter.
She fights her way in. The scales inside
the ostiole scrape her hard to clean
off bacteria and fungi she might
bring into the sterile nursery.
Special teeth on her mandibles and forelegs
let her cut through without ever losing ground.
Her wings and antennae are ripped away
but she has no further need of them.

Once inside the dark nest
her ovipositor places eggs in blooms.
Her young will eat the seeds of these but she
will pollinate others often as she works.
The fig seeds will feed her young while she
ensures the next generation of the tree.

When she's laid her eggs, the fig becomes
a tomb blossom, as her soft body parts
are absorbed by the fruit.
                                    The larvae of
her young may not be alone in this dark
enclave. For other mothers aim
to feed their young on her brood.
Wasps outside the fig locate her eggs
and like a high oil rig drilling in the ocean
with ovipositors many times their body length
push down and place their eggs to hatch
then feast on her living larvae.

When her unmolested offspring morph
their parasitic neighbours morph too
having eaten only half the fig wasps.
Why they curb their hunger is clear—
they must find a way out of the fig
and need the help of their gentle prey.

When the wasps emerge inside the fig
the males, with no life outside these dark
precincts, who have no wings, no eyes, only
rudimentary legs, still find the girls. These
may well be their sisters.
                                        Having mated
the male's final duty is heroic—
to tunnel through the fruit and build
an exit. He guards this door
and soon expires in sun. The females
charge through, fly off to seek a new
receptive fig. The parasite wasps
leave soon after.
                                        Game on again.
All wasps gone, fig ripens fast
becoming delicious to birds, lizards,
monkeys and men.

This interdependence of fig and wasp
is so nicely balanced that figs hold
wider swathe than other plants
with insects that lead mutually
regarding lives, like yuccas and moths
or ants with subterranean fungi
or orchids with euglossine bees whose
sexy shenanigans so moved Darwin.

And what will vegans make of this?
Can they still eat figs, knowing
some mother wasp body parts lay inside?

Most fresh commercial figs are mother free
grown through cuttings in the hand
rather than the aid of wasps.
The dry figs of Smyrna, though, and the fat
wild ones I gorge on in the hills of France, still
carry on like all their nine hundred clan
members throughout the warm world. So vegans
beware the wild figs—and leave them for me.

Janzen, D., How to be a Fig, *Annual Review of Ecology and Systematics 1979*, 10:13–51, doi:10.1146/*annurev*.es.10.110179.000305.

Weiblen, G., How to be a fig wasp, *Annual Review of Entomology 2002*, 47:299–330, doi:10.1146/*annurev*.ento.47.091201.145213.

Male fig wasps sometimes sever the heads of other males to secure their position to mate. *See* Cook, J. M., *et al.,* Fighting in fig wasps: do males avoid killing brothers or do they never meet them? *Ecological Entomology* (3 Sept 2015), doi:10.1111/een.12250; Armoured wasps chop off opponents' heads in brutal fig wars, *New Scientist* (26 Sept 2015), 17.

Long ago and under water

In a lake swim two small fish
side by side in bony armour

their little fins entwined.
He presses his clasper against

her spiny ventral bones that dock
then clutch at him like velcro.

This is their moment, their water
ballet to the tune of progeny.

They are the first of the antiarchs
the first of the placoderms

the first of all the vertebrates
on Earth where the mingling

of egg and sperm takes place
in her inner realms: what we came

to know as sex. They raise their
broods in an underwater palace

in a place that we call Scotland
three hundred fifty million years on.

Morelle, R., Sex 'emerged' in an ancient Scottish lake, bbc.in/2k3XZUR (19 Oct 2014), retrieved 2 Feb 2017.

Long, J.A., *et al.,* Copulation in antiarch placoderms and the origin of gnathostome internal fertilization, *Nature* 517, 196–199 (8 January 2015), doi:10.1038nature13825.

Traumatic matings

When you and I are sea slugs
and we meet on the coral sands
we'll wear living mantles:
coats of billowing colours.

And if we're in the happy
genus *Siphopteron,* among
'unnamed species one' then we'll
be hermaphrodites too, able

to mate with any of our mates.
When a date begins to make
us both feel serious we'll nibble
each other's mantle then settle down

to pump up our penis bulbs and insert
them in each other for a slow
and cosy forty-five minutes.
It's then that we will start to duel.

We'll unsheathe our pointy
penis stylets to puncture each
other's forehead then pump in
prostate fluid full of hormones.

You'll be trying to hack my brain
and make my body play the female
so you can fertilize piles of my
eggs, while I do the same to you.

In the coral seas on the coral
sands when we are hermaphrodite
sea slugs there'll be a little bit of
brain trauma in our every love affair.

Lange, R., *et al.,* Cephalo-traumatic secretion transfer in a hermaphroditic
sea slug, *Proceedings of the Royal Society B* (13 Nov 2013), doi:10.1098/
rspb.2013.2424.

"Mind controlling sea slug stabs its lover in the head," *New Scientist* (16
Nov 2013), 17.

QUARTET WITH PARASITES

The best sort of parasite commands not just
the body but also the brain of its victim.

I

Cordyceps is a fungus whose spore
may fall upon an ant and set that ant
a quest that leads to its demise. Infected
it walks up a plant that is to hand
and finds a spot with the right moisture
in the air. Then at solar noon it locks
its jaws as an ant would never do on leaf
or twig. From this stable platform
Cordyceps ravages the ant's entire
being then erupts from its head to rain
down spores upon its nest mates.

There are thousands of *Cordyceps,*
each tuned to a single species, pruning
its population to fit in life's garden.

II

Toxoplasmois can live in the flesh of most
mammals but needs a cat for sexual
reproduction. Eight spores like bullets
load each *Toxo* cyst. From inside a cat
the cysts go coursing for prey through poo.

They can wait for a year locked and loaded.
If they meet a rodent, the spores hack
its brain. A sane mouse runs from cat
piss pong. Not so a mouse with *Toxo* on
the brain. For such a mouse cat piss is an
irresistible lure, the cat itself a god.
Mouse approaches cat and looks
up into its eye entranced. Cat consumes
Toxo with mouse and the cycle repeats.

Toxo infests our brain too. Like mice we get
self destructive and our reactions slow.
Think motorcycle deaths and car crashes.
Think suicides and schizophrenia. Think
women cheating on husbands and men overly
aggressive. In those with low immune response,
dementia. All these are linked to *Toxoplasmosis*
in our brains. We get the cysts from raw infected
meat—in the land of steak tartar eighty four percent
of the French host *Toxo*— or from unwashed
fruit and veg whose roots reach into soil where
Toxo hides or from our kitty's litter.

III

Sacculina is a barnacle and scourge of crabs.
It's not like the bony pyramids that coat docks
and the hulls of ships. An innocuous teardrop
of cells, the female *Sacculina* smells out
a female crab and lands upon its leg.
She finds where the armour is soft
in the joints and small hairs exit through

minute holes. *Sacculina* injects a hypodermic
here, pumps in a slurry of her cells and subsides.

These cells course to the crab's underside
and grow a knob. From here *Sacculina*
pushes tendrils through the crab
twining around everything including its eye
stalks while avoiding an immune response.
Sacculina grows on nutrients in the crab's
blood until the crab gives up its life to serve
the parasite. No longer does it shed its shell
to grow. This would waste nutrients *Sacculina*
can better use. No longer can the crab reproduce
for *Sacculina* has taken over the hardware.
When a male *Sacculina* teardrop finds a crab
infested with its female, it pumps its blob of cells
into the knob on the belly's bottom where
the female crab's sexual organs were.
His cells enter the she-*Sacculina's*
pulsing vent and begin to make sperm.

A healthy crab will clean algae from her brood
and a *Sacculina* filled crab will take equal care
of the parasite's breeding knob. A healthy crab
when ready to spawn will find a high rock
with swirling current, pump out her eggs
and use her claws to further stir the waters.
Now she does all this for the cloud of parasites
she releases as though her own.

When a female *Sacculina* finds a male crab
she enters as she would a female, hijacks the male

crab's system and, with eyestalks covered in
Sacculina cells, he becomes a female crab replica
devoting all his life and energy to being a factory
for thousands of new parasites.

IV

Contemplating another parasite, a wasp whose
larvae eat living caterpillars from inside out
Darwin, devout enough to have considered
the ministry, wondered if the Christian God exists.

Cordyceps

Costandi, M., Zombie ant parasitic fungus castrated by hyperparasitic
fungus (3 May 2012), bit.ly/2jDfSqc, retrieved 1 Feb 2017.

Attenborough, D., Cordyceps: attack of the killer fungi – *Planet Earth* (3
Nov 2008), bit.ly/2jwb7TU, retrieved 1 Feb 2017.

Toxoplasmosis

Wilcox, C., Toxoplasma's Dark Side: The Link Between the Parasite and
Suicide, *Scientific American* (4 July 2012), bit.ly/2ksiISX, retrieved 1 Feb
2017.

Zimmer, C., A Common Parasite Reveals Its Strongest Asset: Stealth,
New York Times (20 June 2006), nyti.ms/2jwbTjL, retrieved 12 Feb 2016.

Coccaro, E.F., *et al., Toxoplasma gondii* Infection: Relationship With Aggression in Psychiatric Subjects, Journal of Clinical Psychiatry (Mar 2016), bit.ly/2kVRykl, retrieved 1 Feb 2017.

SACCULINA

Carl Zimmer's buoyant and scary book on parasites must be read by everyone interested in nature. The chapter on Sacculina is an opera darker than Bluebeard's Castle: Zimmer, C., *Parasite Rex: Inside the Bizarre World of Nature's Most Dangerous Creatures* (New York: Free Press, 2000).

PARASITIC WASPS

Darwin wrote, "I cannot persuade myself that a beneficent & omnipotent God would have designedly created the Ichneumonidæ [parasitic wasps] with the express intention of their feeding within the living bodies of caterpillars, or that a cat should play with mice." Darwin, C., from a letter to Asa Gray, 22 May 1860, bit.ly/2kqTXac, retrieved 1 Feb 2017.

Wasps employ the most up to date techniques of genetic manipulation in securing a meal for their growing larvae. They use bracoviruses, which they have tamed over the last 100 million years to the point that the viruses can no longer reproduce on their own. The virus turns off the immune system of the caterpillar the wasp lays her eggs in, so that the caterpillar's system cannot attack the wasp's larva as it develops and eats the host. A different virus species is employed by each of the thousands of species of braconid wasps, each species of wasp in turn parasitizing its own separate butterfly or moth target species. *See* If viruses transfer wasp genes into butterflies, are they GM? *New Scientist* (17 Sept 2015), bit.ly/1JeviWO, retrieved 1 Feb 2017.

The wasps also use gene splicing techniques to create transgenic viruses, and the genetic modifications sometimes move into the butterfly or moth genome (e.g., Monarchs), perhaps when a wasp parasitizes a caterpillar of the wrong species and it survives to pass on the viral genes. *See* Gasmi, L., *et al.,* Recurrent Domestication by Lepidoptera of Genes from Their Parasites Mediated by Bracoviruses, *PLoS Genetics* (17 Sept 2015), doi:10.1371/journal.pgen.1005470.

The dead fish of Chad

Let me tell you a story
about the dead fish of Chad.

They fossilized at the bottom of a great
lake that evaporated into Sahara.

Now their bones and scales
are phosphorous of a special kind

like bonemeal. Resting in sand
in the world's windiest place

the fossils are particle by particle
scoured to dust then lofted high to fly

the Atlantic with the Aeolian swarm.
Over the teeming Amazon

the fossil dust falls from the sky
like a fine and precious rain

like something medieval alchemists
could only scheme and write about

like something Venetian traders
would have sailed their galleys for

like something new age Gaians
must feel a special reverence toward

like incense the ancient Egyptians
paid fortunes to import from

the land of Punt to propitiate deities
on whom daily life depends.

When at last fossil particles
meet forest floor they fertilize it.

Since the world depends upon this forest
it depends on the fine grained dust of Chad.

One day of course desert wind
will have its way and the Sahara's

unremitting sand grains one on one
will smooth the scales and bones away.

And so researchers who discovered
this secret ingredient in the nourishing

dust are on a plane to measure
the balance in our dead fish account

and I'm wondering how much poor Chad
should be charging for this dust of life.

Amos, J., Ancient African fish dust nourishes Amazon, bbc.in/2kw5Ef2
(24 Sept 2014), retrieved 9 Feb 2015.

Hudson-Edwards, K.A., *et al.,* Solid-phase phosphorous speciation in
Saharan Bodele Depression dusts and source sediments, *Chemical Geology*
384, 16–26 (25 Sept 2014), doi.org/10.1016/j.chemgeo.2014.06.014.

The lodger

In zoology there's a name from the Latin
for making your living as a lodger:
iniquilinism. The cuckoo bee
plays at this game. Furry with a touch
of iridescence on the wings,
it's a handsome five millimetres
when it comes unannounced to the home
of a bee we know better, say a solitary
bee's adobe nest tube.

                    The cuckoo bee
lays her eggs in the host's brood cell.
The young cuckoo hatches and wakes
to eat the pollen stored by the host
for its own. Next as the main course it
eats the juicy larvae, progeny of its host,
before buzzing off to seek new digs
with full larder. Several thousand species
of bee have taken up the lodger's life.

This poem was sparked by a centrefold in *New Scientist,* "Buzz of the Cuckoo Bee," *New Scientist* (2 Nov 2013), 27.

Bogush, P., *et al.,* Generalist cuckoo bees (Hymenoptera: Apoidea: *Sphecodes*) are species-specialist at the individual level, *Behavioral Ecology and Sociobiology* 60:422–429 (July 2006), doi:10.1007/s00265–006–0182–4.

LIKE MILKSHAKES

Venoms are distinguished from poisons
by being proteinacious secretions
mixed in special glands and by their
active mode of delivery through wounds
inflicted by fangs and other special structures.

Of the four great classes of arthropods
just one lacked any impresario of venoms.
While spiders, insects and the centipede
group of myriapods are all famous for
their venoms, some of intricate design,

only crustaceans went without. That's
all changed with a discovery about
remipedes, whose handle sounds like
an ancient Greek playwright, or a hero
in the Iliad, one who's loyal but not

in the front lines with Ajax. Instead
they're pale, rare, blind crustaceans
at home in pools in sinkhole caves
scattered about Mexico and Central
America with a few outliers elsewhere.

Imagine a centipede swimming
with oarlike legs and you have their habitus.
Scientists lit postprandial remipedes
with their lamps and found them discarding
empty shrimp shells like burger wrappers.

Looking closer, remipedes have
little needles on their front claws
to inject venom that paralyzes then
digests the victim, allowing remipedes
to drink their prey, as one researcher
put it, like milkshakes.

Of the seventy thousand species
of known crustacean, remipedes stand
alone for now in bearing venom.

Kaplan, M., First venomous crustacean discovered, *Nature* (22 Oct 2013), doi:10.1038/nature.2013.13985.

Von Reumont, B. *et al.,* The First Venomous Crustacean Revealed by Transcriptomics and Functional Morphology: Remipede Venom Glands Express a Unique Toxin Cocktail Dominated by Enzymes and a Neurotoxin, *Molecular Biology and Evolution* 31 (1): 48–58 (2014), doi:10.1093/molbev/mst199.

The first stanza of this poem tracks the language of the investigators, showing how rewarding it can be to browse journals.

Hungry daughters

Were Kafka to script your
waking one day and you
gazing down discover

a pea aphid is your new form
you'd be the daughter of
a mother without father.

You're a clone in a lineage
of female clones stretching back
to the aphid uber mother.

When rainfall is low and plant
juices less luxuriant you'll drink,
if you can, the body fluids

of your siblings. And if you're young
and very hungry you'll gang
up on your mother, puncture

her to drain her body dry
and normally she'll not resist.

Marshall, M., Baby vampire aphids drink parents' blood, *Science* (9 Nov 2013), doi:10.1016/S0262–4079(13)62628–7.

The rolling of the dungball

When a scarab finds fresh dung, marvellous.
It is a connoisseur, and crafts a globe
to push down a hole so the entire
family can consume the gift.

Due to the rolling of the dungball
Egypt knew the beetle sacred, an avatar of Ra
who rolls Sun through sky each day.
When scarab sculpts her ball, she climbs on
top and seems to dance in triumph. We've
now learned the inner meaning of the dance:
to find bearings for the job of rolling.
Should she slip and circle back to dungheap
another scarab will try to steal her prize.

Only birds and people were known to use
sidereal navigation. On a moonless night
she looks up with her gem-like compound
eyes at the soft wide sweep of Milky Way
and takes our stellar plane as her map.

To know this is a complete answer
to feeling bereft, without purpose
or alone in the universe.

Dacke, M., *et al.,* Dung Beetles Use the Milky Way for Orientation,
Current Biology (18 Feb 2013), 298–300, doi:10.1016/j.cub.2012.12.034.

HEAD OF GLASS

A lineage of linear jellies
bears a name like a sea wind:
siphonophore.

Their colonies pulse through
the world ocean to sting
and eat what comes along.

Enter the barreleye fish, known
from damaged specimens dragged
up for decades, then videoed in
Monterey Bay a few years back.

Contrary to all our inbuilt
frames of reference this small
dark fish from eight hundred metres
down has a fully transparent head

its tubular green eyes tucked
safely inside. They point up to look
through the clean clear domed
glassy skull (and can speed rotate
to see what's before the mouth).

The barreleye lurks dark and quiet
waiting for siphonophores
to drift overhead.

To steal their food
it then darts up with eyes wide open
shielded from responding stings
remaining entirely clear headed.

Harmon, K., The Clear Headed Fish, *Scientific American* (26 Feb 2009), bit.ly/2jVx3nA, retrieved 1 Feb 2017.

"Researchers Solve Mystery of Deep Sea Fish with Tubular Eyes and Transparent Head," Monterey Bay Aquarium Research Institute (23 Feb 2009), bit.ly/1MCN00G, retrieved 1 Feb 2017.

FRINGED WITH TEETH

I've never met an arachnid
I didn't like. With birds of prey
they're famous carnivores. Spiders
have caught my interest most
but scorpions have much to recommend
them. Whip scorpions, whose gang
name is vinegaroon, are bruisers.
In place of a stinger they've got
a spigot they use to blast you with acid
before having you for lunch.

There's a whip scorpion though
the delicate member of the gang
that's just a millimetre long
and keeps to the dark of Slovakia's
Ardovská Cave. These tiny, flimsy-
armoured, pale and fragile arachnids
have mouth parts, known in the business
as chelicerae, shaped like forceps
and fringed with comb-like teeth.

Cyanobacteria also live in the cave,
members of the oldest living group
on Earth, known from fossils at life's
dawn. Though they make their living
from sunlight they're adaptable enough
to dwell in caves and inside Nubian rock.

The Ardovská whip scorpions use their
nicely fashioned mouthparts to scrape bacteria
from living rock then eat them, the only
arachnids that don't eat other animals.
Turns out there is a vegan even in this gang.

Smrž, J., *et al.,* Microwhip Scorpions (Palpigradi) Feed on Heterotrophic
Cyanobacteria in Slovak Caves – A Curiosity among Arachnida,
PLoSOne (16 Oct 2013), doi:10.1371/journal.pone.0075989.

E.O. Wilson's favourite ant

I cannot interview the world's best known
ant expert, said Penny Sarchet, without asking:
do you have a favourite? E.O. Wilson replied:

I do. It's an ant called *Thaumatomyrmex*. In all
my travels, I've only seen three. They're very rare.
It has teeth on jaws that look like a pitchfork.
The teeth are extremely long, and when it closes
the jaws, they overlap. In at least one species
the teeth actually meet behind the head.

So what does this monster eat?
What does it use those teeth for?
I just had to know so I sent an appeal
out to younger experts in the field,
particularly in South America
where these ants are found.

Eventually they discovered the answer: it feeds
on polyxenid millipedes. These millipedes have
soft bodies, but they're bristling all over like a
porcupine. So the ant drives a spike right through
the bristles and nails it. And what we hadn't noticed
is that the ant also has thick little brushes on some
of its limbs, and members of the colony use these
to scrub the bristles off—like cleaning a chicken—
before dividing it up. That's my favourite.

This is a found poem. Some scientists make good listening. E.O. Wilson speaks so lyrically about his ant it needs to be savoured straight. The original may be found at: Sarchet, P., Don't let Earth's tapestry unravel: Interview with E.O. Wilson, *New Scientist* (24 Jan 2015), 29.

Eminent Britons

The ice has come and gone in green
humped Britain, once home to mammoths
trumpeting their love, to prowling cats
with sabre teeth and irritable rhinoceri.

While these charismatic actors played
out their megafaunal roles, small
persistence ruled the roots. Members
of an ancient cryptic taxa roamed
unmolested in the water underground.

These creatures, stygobites to you,
family name *Niphargus,*
survived the Pleistocine blithe
in their dark homeland, the drama above
no more than an interval in their story
that runs through nineteen million
years of shrimplike life and continues
right beneath our feet.

Niphargus are the oldest living denizens
in this land comfortably seen by naked
eye. They are thus the most eminent
of Britons, whose manor is greater in extent
than the monarch's. They also live
in Ireland, a memory of former unity.

McInerney, C., *et al.,* The Ancient Britons: groundwater fauna survived extreme climate change over tens of millions of years across NW Europe, *Molecular Ecology* (20 Feb 2014), doi:10.1111/mec.12664.

Aerial wars

One day when I was a boy
Miss Gray confided a thing
of great moment about
the ear mites of moths.

It would be best to hear
with both ears
when you're a succulent morsel
and the clicks that precede
the bat's swoop come
from any direction at all.

When you're a hawkmoth
you can fly faster than most
birds and turn like a dancer.
Your ultrasonic hearing catches
the vector of the bat's attack so
you can take action to evade.

Mites might trouble you though.
The most interesting ones
live in your ears and build colonies
in the aural canals. To reach your
blood they puncture your
tympanum bringing deafness.

The marvel is they will never
infest both ears, so you can
always hear the bat coming
and their village in your
aural canal stays safe.

How these canniest of mites
concentrate their cluster in one
ear only is still a mystery.

I'd guess the pioneer mites,
hopping from a flower
while the moth sips nectar,
leave a pheromonal trail so
the next mites know the way to
a cozy spot to sink a proboscis.

And if you are the moth
there is also this:
You can zap bats
with sonic blasts
from your genitals.

When you hear the bat ping
to find you in the dark just
strike your organs to send a
strong pulse of ultrasound
back, threatening the bat
in his own hunting dialect

then slip down from the unsafe skies
to a sheltering rock or bush
until your good ear tells you
that now it's safe again
to search out the nectar of the night.

Treat, A.E., Mites from Noctuid Moths, *Journal of the Lepidopterists' Society* 21, 169 (1967).

Watson, T., Hawkmoths zap bats with sonic blasts from their genitals, *Nature News* (3 July 2013), doi:10.1038/nature.2013.13333.

Abdulla, S., The aerial war of moths and bats, *Nature News* (1 Apr 1999), doi:10.1038/news990401-5.

PENIS ENVY

A new group of insects
has been found and its
females, though unlikely
to have read Freud, are
even less likely
to suffer penis envy.

In four species of *Neotrogla*
the female has a penis-
like organ with sharp spines
she shoves into her male's
vagina. It acts like a vacuum
hoovering up his sperm.

She pins her partner for seventy
hours of straight love sucking.
The guy's sperm comes in packets
with lots of protein and she
may be keen on these because
their love nest is the fasting
environment of dark caves.

Nuzzo, R., Female insect uses spiky penis to take charge, *Nature News* (7 Apr 2014), doi:10.1038/nature.2014.15064.

THE NEWS ABOUT NEANDERTHALS

With a Victorian sense of self regard
we have fashioned them into an Other:
durable brutes, slow witted and dumb,
pitted against our forebears, best wiped out.
Below the level of the ordinary scandals
and disasters, several story lines are emerging
about our Homo cousins the Neanderthals.

Turns out they adorned themselves with
feathers and buried their dead in well made
graves from Israel to France. Excavations in
Italy show they built pleasant work-live studios,
with separate spaces to butcher meat, store
supplies, cook and sleep and near the entrance
set up workshops to craft new tools.

Our ability to extract and read ancient DNA
has grown. Modern Europeans and Asians get up
to four percent of our DNA from Neanderthals.
We must have known them close and well.

My favourite news is about language.
It's down to a hyoid bone
discovered in 1989 to hold
the tongue's root, poised in us
but not in chimps for speech.
New computer modelling shows
that in Neanderthals the hyoid position
should have made them eloquent as we.

They shared the world with us until they
disappeared some thirty thousand years ago
from their final range in Spain.
Some say we not only slept with
but ate them. Others that even though
their brains were bigger than ours
they had such good eyes much brain power
was used for sight, so they could see us
coming for miles but couldn't out-think us,
the myopic killers. Others say
we out-competed or exterminated them
like we do other indigenous groups.

While we don't know their ending, we
are learning they were more articulate
and artistic than we had thought, had
their rituals and separate work stations.
Is our feeling they were brutes a race
memory justifying our extermination
of them? Have we suppressed knowing
they were warm friendly people
we feasted and then slept with?

It's easy now to imagine a Neanderthal
mother's lullaby and her shaggy swain's
whispered endearments. These cousins
of ours, like cousins you've not seen
for years then meet at a family Christmas,
are turning out to be far more accomplished
than we thought.

D'Anastasio, R., *et al.,* Micro-Biomechanics of the Kebara 2 Hyoid and Its Implications for Speech in Neanderthals, *PLoSOne* 8(12): e82261 (18 Dec 2013), doi:10.1371/journal.pone.0082261.

Pearce, E., *et al.,* New insights into differences in brain organization between Neanderthals and anatomically modern humans, *Proceedings of the Royal Society B* (13 Mar 2013), doi:10.1098/rspb.2013.0168.

"New Evidence Suggests Neanderthals Organized their Living Space," *Science Daily* (3 Dec 2013), bit.ly/2jwbkqk, retrieved 1 Feb 2017.

See also Jaubert, J., *et al.,* Early Neanderthal constructions deep in Bruniquel Cave in southwestern France, *Nature* (2 June 2016), doi:10.1038/nature18291.

CONQUERING EARTH

We were unpromising hominids
in our savannah forest nursery. What
then let us conquer Earth and make it
our safe home, a paradise we now
steward in its robust fragility?

It's a gene driven tale. Our early forebears
were large and territorial, rich material
for evolution's deft revising.

About 80 million years ago we took
to trees, giving us hands and feet
good for grasping. Our brain grew and
binocular vision in full colour came as
we relied more on sight and less on smell
than most mammals. When we later
dropped to ground we walked on two
legs and freed our hands to throw and
craft points of spear and arrow.

Our Promethean moment came and we
learned fire. We made campsites, and these
were our first human nests. We became
eager for meat and learned to cook it.
As campfires burned we looked out
at the world together. We linked
attention to cooperate in killing and
fending off attack. We watched our own

mental states and knew that others shared
them. Our inner realm connected
with the inner realm of others and so laid
foundations of love and loneliness.

As life's next great leap we achieved
language, whose symbols, now
more intimate than our blood, let us share
handsome facts, pose questions that
lead to insight and above all else tell stories.

It built the stage where we rehearse
future meetings (in our need to plan for
them) and past engagements (in our need
to plumb them). Building this space
inside our head was done before we
walked out of Africa. We've been chatting
and obsessing our way to who we are
for at least 60 thousand years by now.

What made us aggressive meat eating
apes with hearts of gold? We know
ourselves as dual, as good and as corrupt,
greedy and generous, our inner landscape
the yin and yang later called the Tao.

What's the reason, every time we have
smoothed our inner fields, they will be
turned over for both weeds and flowers?

Natural selection is the cause, playing
two handed evolutionary jazz on
the keyboard of our genome. The left
hand is individual selection, sometimes
dubbed the selfish gene. It plays the bass
lends darkness to our theme and is
the source of our conniving and aggression
our rapacity and Lady Macbeth's lines.

The right hand is group selection. It plays the
harmonies, the tunes of hope, the love songs
and redemption songs, what we see as light.
Compassion for others, self sacrifice and
group feeling all flow from this source. So
too getting along on a packed commuter train.
Otherwise, we'd murder each other before
we got to our suburban stop, as would a train
full of chimps, if you laid on such a trip.

Selection at the level of the group shapes
just those species who often focus on
others; turn your mind to ants and
honeybees, naked mole rats and us.

When we lit our first campfires
group selection blazed too. We
learned to cooperate as our tribe
vied with neighbouring tribes.
The team player was born. Tribes who
played best won the world. E. O. Wilson
states an iron rule that gives much hope.

It goes like this: selfish individuals beat
altruistic ones but a group of altruists
always beats a troupe of the selfish.

Our campfires are now board rooms and
parliaments and our nests now condos
and shanty towns. Knowing the basis
of our dual nature and accepting it is
who we are, both sides of us arising
in every generation, the challenge
presents itself: can we gain a new
maturity and so survive in a world
healthy enough to want to call home?

I have been following E. O. Wilson's work since the publication of his
Sociobiology: The New Synthesis (Boston: Harvard University Press 1975).
That book was my refuge during the summer of '76 when I lived in a walk-
up with bathroom down the hall on Bleeker Street in Greenwich Village,
before I started law school. Wilson does foundational research then rises
to general theory with clarity and aplomb. This poem tries to capture the
essence of the argument laid out in *The Social Conquest of Earth* (New
York: Liveright 2013).

A CENTURY OF GORGING

In Africa they evolved wary of us
as we came down from trees
and learned to hunt them
the big mammals. Then we
streamed north and east and
the great ones fell one by one
in a slow moving fire of extinction
that followed us as we went.

We crossed the land bridge into North America
when there were still camels and cheetahs,
big-as-truck ground sloths, lions and
sabre toothed cats, short faced bear
and dire wolves, mammoths and mastodons,
not one but three kinds of wild horse.

Within a little while they were gone.
None had seen us apes before so
when we crept and raised our sharp
tipped spears death came unexpected.

This blaze ran everywhere out
of Africa just behind the march of human
feet. Some scientists hold tight
their sceptical duty. It could
have been climate change, they say,
or infections like those the white men
brought as gifts to the Indians. For new
evidence, repair to the Antipodes.

As we moved from island to island
across Polynesia we ate our way through
some thousand species of endemic birds
whose bones we piled in our villages
as they disappeared in the wild.

From there we made it to New Zealand
in the fourteenth century and found it
full of moas, giant ostrich like creatures
some weighing as much as five men.

So handy were these big moas
that the first of us to arrive
ate them thoroughly
eggs, young, breeding pairs
and kept piling high their bones
until after a century of gorging
they were no more. (Now tell me

wouldn't you have done the same?
They probably tasted real good, like
chicken.) Still the sceptics said, perhaps
there was some other cause, maybe
the moas were ready to snuff the candle.

Now at last we have a clear report.
An elegant look at DNA from moa
bones of the last 4000 years
shows the great birds thriving
in their prime when we showed up.

Then they disappeared like snow
in a bakery. The verdict: we were
the perp. And what of all those
extinctions of the great ones
who roamed the continents when
we arrived amidst their numbers?

Our ancestors lived no more
in harmony with nature than we.
We were not different then
had no more forethought
just slower tools for killing.

If any of us in any age get into harmony
with nature it will be by growing up
not going back.
                    Oh and those native
great herds of wild horses in
North America were extinguished
by our indigenous ancestors. Who for
that reason were on foot when
the Spaniards dropped by.

M. Allentoft, M., *et al.,* Extinct New Zealand megafauna were not in decline before human colonization, *Proceedings of the National Academy of Sciences* 111, 4922–4927 (10 Feb 2014), doi:10.1073/pnas.1314972111.

Bartlett, L., *et al.,* Robustness despite uncertainty: regional climate data reveal the dominant role of humans in explaining global extinctions of Late Quaternary megafauna, *Ecography* (29 July 2015), doi:10.1111/ecog.01566.

Morell, V., Why Did New Zealand's Moas Go Extinct? *Science* (17 Mar 2014), bit.ly/2k3MEUA, retrieved 2 Feb 2017.

"Dead as the moa," *The Economist* (14 Sept. 2013), econ.st/2lo8h5Q, retrieved 2 Feb 2017.

A BULLETIN FROM OUR BRANCH

News from our branch of the tree
is that chimps are the only other
primates who kill their neighbours.
Murder runs free in them like us
and the blood that we both let.

I study the photo of an alpha male
pinned down and screaming
as the males around him work
methodically at his death.
That they were chimps
made it no less familiar.

Lebensraum whipped good Germans
into frenzy. In Rwanda lack of land
may have been a root. In chimps
it appears to be the same: The more
males born into the band the more
neighbours the band of chimps will kill
to get more food and mates. They too
buy living space with conspecific blood.
The numbers they kill are proportional
to those we kill when we live in tribes.

As climate warms and groups of people
need to move while population swells
our genetic ground of violence
won't leave my mind alone.

Webb, J., Murder 'comes naturally' to chimpanzees (18 Sept 2014), bbc.
in/2kXE9cf, retrieved 13 Feb 2016.

Wilson, M., *et al.,* Lethal aggression in *Pan* is better explained by adaptive
strategies than human impacts, *Nature* 513, 414–417 (18 Sept 2014),
doi:10.1038/nature13727.

WARM WET AND QUANTUM

o and 1 line up in strings of bits
to make our current world.
Bits are off or on but never both;
qubits live different. These quantum
bits play both parts at once.
Were they the soul of your
machine (and stayed coherent)
you'd flash through calculations
side by side in shoals and answers
would slip out in seconds
that now would take us aeons.

Any wonder Google and IBM are
betting on qubits? But they can't
yet control ten at once
and to herd their lonely band
for briefest must kill the heat
and chill them near zero's absolute.

In jungle heat, plants are always at it.
When I last looked into photosynthesis
a dozen years ago, its inner devices
were obscure. Now we know plants
compute in quantum ways
in systems warm, wet and turbulent.

Life's most important molecule after
DNA, chlorophyll, harvests light.
An atom of magnesium lies in its heart.
When a photon running from the Sun
knocks an electron from the atom
the work begins. This energy bearing
electron, now an *exciton*, must reach
the *reaction centre* fast to store not
lose its pulse. We thought the exciton
took a random walk to get there. Such
a walk is wasteful though, and the energy
transfers with almost no loss at all.

Turns out the exciton takes a *quantum*
walk. It peers ahead at the energy
landscape and scans all paths at
once. Best route found, the exciton
gains the goal and stores its energy safely.

Impossible they said. It's clear though.
Photosynthesis nourishes everyone
by amplifying quantum events in
the warm, wet, turbulent inner world
of leaves into most of the biomass on Earth.

Al-Khalili, J., & McFadden, J., *Life on the Edge: The Coming Age of Quantum Biology* (London: Black Swan 2014), 141–183.

Engel, G.S., *et al.,* Evidence for wavelike energy transfer through quantum coherence in photosynthetic systems, *Nature* 446, 782–86 (12 Apr 2007), doi:10.1038/nature05678. *See also* Calhoun, T.R., *et al.,* Quantum coherence enabled determination of the energy landscape in light-harvesting complex II, *Journal of Physical Chemistry B,* 113:51, 16291–95 (20 Oct 2009), doi:10.1021/jp908300c.

Google and IBM hope to manage hundreds of qbits by around 2020. *See* Gibney, E., Silicon quantum computers take shape in Australia, *Nature* 553, 448–49 (26 May 2016), doi:10.1038/533448a.

New equilibria

We go into the future
        incrementally
like a coconut grows
        or a dynamical system,
gaining energy in the synergy
        of its parts, moves
to the edge of its stable state
        and without warning
finds a new equilibrium
        and we find the covers
of our habits slipped. It could
        be a relationship
ended or a blue lake we swam
        in eutrophied.

        In the hundred thousand
years before our memory,
        the Earth has gone
up and down by ten degrees
        several times,
the kind of change now, if up,
        that would goodbye us.
These earlier adjustments may have
        taken little as a decade.
Incrementally leads you to the edge
        and then it's over.

Conkling, P., *et al., The Fate of Greenland: Lessons from Abrupt Climate Change* (Cambridge: MIT Press 2011), 16; 73.

Alley, R.B., *et al.,* Abrupt Climate Change, *Science* 299, 2005–2010 (28 Mar 2003), doi:10.1126/science.1081056.

The rules of loss

Roads are a harmless convenience
in the story of our culture or more
than that by now, a necessity that
lets our cars and vans, our lorries
and shining pantechnicons flow like
corpuscles along metalled ways we
liken to the blood stream by calling
them arterial. This blood stream
of our social body is as needed for
the life we share as our own corpuscular
highways to our daily living.

In the rainforest rethink this: cutting
a road begins the unmaking of the web
of life and its many creatures who have
differentiated so disproportionate
to cooler climes we have not fully
understood their commune life,
its members, how they might help us
in the next phase of our evolution
or the cause of their extravagance.

A road in the rainforest is like a surgeon's
knife when you lie anaesthetised upon
the table: it cuts through living substance.
There the image ends for a surgeon's cut
can lead to healing while a road's may
never heal. That's long been thought
but now is proven in the longest

ecological study ever done spanning
five continents and thirty-five years.

In the sixties Wilson and MacArthur said
if you want to know what happens
to a piece of forest when you cut it off
look at islands. Those are much less rich
in species and recruit far fewer new ones.

So Lovejoy and others separated patches
of forest and watched minutely through
the years. The loss begins at once.

In just a year the forest fragment
may lose a fifth of its mammals, birds,
its insects and plants. At ten years
the loss can stretch to half and at twenty
three quarters of the forest's former life
may be gone forever. The loss plays out
longer yet, paying off an extinction debt
booked when forest became fragment.

The half-life of plutonium-239, the time
it takes to lose half its radioactivity, is
twenty-four thousand years. The half-life
of a forest fragment, the time it takes
to lose half its species richness, only ten.

These rules of loss apply most liberally:
to grasslands, northern moss, and temperate
woods, but matter most in rainforest
since that's where most things live.

Slicing by road causes loss but
the road also invites guests.
Illegal goldminers bring their poison,
swidden farmers their tree burning,
cattle ranchers their pastures, loggers
fell swathes, and wildfires follow them
to speed the loss, and reach for
the horizon both sides the road's ribbon.

Around the world, three fourths of forest
lies near as a kilometre to a road
so death by fragmentation is broadly
underway. Only the Amazon and Congo
keep ultra blocks inviolate. These are
threatened too. We plan twenty-five
million new kilometres of road in the next
few decades, mostly in the developing
world, where the rainforest is.

Ecologists are outlining how new roads
can be laid for most benefit with least
harm, preserving the natural systems
we will always rely on.

Reporting on their 35 year, five continent study, the authors write, "Across experiments, average loss was >20% after 1 year, >50% after 10 years, and is still increasing in the longest time series measured (more than two decades)." Haddad, N.M, *et al.,* Habitat fragmentation and its lasting impact on Earth's ecosystems, *Science Advances* Vol. 1, no. 2, e1500052 (20 Mar 2015), doi:10.1126/sciadv.1500052.

Nijhuis, M., What Roads Have Wrought, *The New Yorker* (20 Mar 2015).

Laurance, W., *et al.,* A Global Strategy for Roadbuilding, *Nature* 513, 229–232 (27 Aug 2014), doi:10.1038/nature13717.

MacArthur, R. H., and Wilson, E.O., *The Theory of Island Biogeography* (Princeton: Princeton University Press 1967).

Spat

Oyster spat have forty-eight hours
to build armour and get eating.
When seawater's sweet it's easy
but increasing acid sweeps away
the minerals shell-building's based on.
Unless the spat can beat the clock they
drift into sea space alone and dead.

Spat have been dying in droves in
bays off America's West Coast.
So oystermen now throw antacid in
the souring seas, against the carbon
dioxide dissolving down from air.

Colder water holds more, think
champagne, whose bubble CO_2 turns
to carbonic acid on your tongue as it
does in the fluid sea. The acid breaks
up a family of carbonate minerals
needed to craft skeletons and shells

and will dissolve these direct
when concentrations go high.
Since Queen Victoria, oceans have
obliged by soaking up forty percent
of global warming's carbon and
ninety percent of its heat.

Some waters have turned from
nursery to harm. Take sea butterflies,
aka pteropods, the most numerous
animals you don't know, free swimming
snails small and beautiful of form.
They eat microscopic plankton and become
key nodes in the food web, devoured
in turn by birds and whales, herring
and salmon. In the California Current
and Southern Ocean, their shells are melting.

Corals will feel their skeletons dissolve
and fish will be scathed. Breathing
is harder in warmer seas that hold
less oxygen for gills. Acid harms
sperm, eggs and larvae. Those in
tropical seas who cannot swim
to colder waters with the cod
will let go of a less gentle planet.

Some algae will come out ahead
fertilized by the changes. Among them
are the poisonous bloomers who this
year floated a scum from Alaska
to Mexico that claimed the lives of thirty
whales, and much else unknown to us.

The Earth speaks to us in the grammar
of science. What it's saying about the oceans
isn't welcome. Will jellyfish rule? It's not yet
clear. Squid? Their larvae too are sensitive
to acid, as is the chemistry of their blood.

By century's end the seas will be sour
as they've been since the dinosaurs. It was
a long time then, more than a hundred
thousand years, till the acid dropped
and carbonates came back free
for the taking. And it will be that long again.

DeVries, T., et al., Recent increase in oceanic carbon uptake driven by weaker upper-ocean overturning, *Nature* 542, 215 (9 Feb 2017), doi:10.1038/nature21068.

Gattuso, J.T., *et al.,* Contrasting futures for ocean and society from different anthropogenic CO2 emissions scenarios, *Science* 349, 6243 (3 July 2015), doi:10.1126/science.aac4722.

An Updated Synthesis of the Impacts of Ocean Acidification on Marine Biodiversity, UNEP Secretariat of the Convention on Biological Diversity (2014).

Grossman, E., Northwest Oyster Die-offs Show Ocean Acidification Has Arrived, *Yale Environment 360* (21 Nov 2011), retrieved 13 Feb 2016.

Fitzer, S.C., *et al.,* Biomineral shell formation under ocean acidification: a shift from order to chaos, *Scientific Reports* 6: 21076 (2016), doi:10.1038/srep21076.

"Ocean acidification killing oysters by inhibiting shell formation" (6 Nov 2013), bit.ly/2khzWAl, retrieved 1 Feb 2017.

CHIROPTERANS

As dusk embraces mountains
in my French retreat, I worry for
chiropterans, the bats. For the last

few weeks an Ebola outbreak, the largest
ever, has been killing West Africans.
Today researchers announced

they've found fruit bats are a reservoir
where the virus hides and waits. How long
before we start killing all the bats

who sweep insects from the skies and spread
the seeds of trees and other needed plants?
Bats are fifty million years older than we

and in their glad variance are a quarter
of all mammal species. Bats react to
pockets of space in the forest mosaic.

Those with broad wings work the dense
canopy while narrow winged ones deploy
in open areas. We cut down forest

and push them into contact. So now
a flock of flying foxes may roost in
the tree shading a pigsty and half eaten

fruit fall to round off an eager porker's
breakfast, giving the ambitious virus
its chance to jump to a species we live

with like family. Then too we eat bushmeat.
Street markets sell bats, some picked up
off the forest floor and teeming with virus.

Whatever our next move, I feel for the bats.

Scientists have known for some years that bats could act as reservoirs. *See* Leroy, E. M., *et al.,* Fruit bats as reservoirs of Ebola virus, *Nature* 438, 575–576 (1 Dec 2005), doi:10.1038/438575a.

For a discussion of how viruses use reservoirs, *see* David Quammen's superb treatment of the subject in *Spillover: Animal Infections and the Next Human Pandemic* (London: Bodley Head 2012).

On the place of bats in the forest scheme *see* Forsyth, A., *Nature of the Rainforest* (Ithaca: Zona Tropical 2008).

Even without concerns about viral reservoirs, people habitually wipe out colonies of bats. *See* http://www.batcon.org/why-bats/bats-are/bats-are-threatened.

Count those lost

When biologists looked at twelve thousand kinds
of flowering plants (of the tribe of three hundred
thousand) they found the majority, sixty-eight
percent, already threatened or endangered.

The world is going through history's third mass coral
bleaching right now. And listen to this. Over just
the last forty years we've lost half the wild animals
on land and sea the world was home to.

We may lose half all *species* by century's end.
This Sixth Great Extinction, our most characteristic
achievement, is down to our hard wiring. I can
love you and decimate creatures at once.

This is our life
this our unwitting
this our challenge.

When we're sick we take care of ourselves.
When at war we motivate ourselves.
While killing life can we change ourselves
or just our actions, enough?

On the loss of plants *see* Buchman, S.L., Our Vanishing Flowers, *New York Times* (16 Oct 2015), nyti.ms/1M75pKn, retrieved 1 Feb 2017.

On coral bleaching *see* Witze A., Corals worldwide hit by bleaching, *Nature News* (8 October 2015), doi:10.1038/nature.2015.18527.

On the loss of wild animals *see* Carrington, D., Earth has lost half of its wildlife in the past forty years, *The Guardian* (30 Sept 2014), bit.ly/1vrStsU, retrieved 5 March 2016.

On the loss of up to half of all species *see* Extinction Crisis, *The Center for Biological Diversity,* bit.ly/1DlG1j4, retrieved 1 Feb 2017.

On the Sixth Extinction *see* Ceballos, G., *et al.,* Accelerated modern human–induced species losses: Entering the sixth mass extinction, *Science Advances* Vol. 1, no. 5 (19 Jun 2015), doi:10.1126/sciadv.1400253.

Coelacanths among us

Who doesn't love coelacanths?
At four hundred million years, among
the oldest of our compeers.

Resplendent in purple flecked with white
their inner life moves at the metabolic
pace of a sarabande not a rap tune.

The coelacanths among us remember
in their bodies the time when life
explored the multi-dimensions of Fish.

They take refuge by day in deepwater
caves of intricate design and the clear cold
water their small gills need to breathe.

By night they drop down into chasms
to drift hunt, letting the currents match them
with such prey as cuttlefish and conger eel.

Their body clocks move so stately
romance starts at nineteen
and life stretches out to a hundred.

A mother carries her pup for three years
before giving her live birth, the longest time
of all things backboned.

We thought they'd
moved from sea to fossil drawer till
1938, when a fisherman off South Africa

pulled the great survivor up alive.
Where do coelacanths find their refugia
and deep cold water full of prey?

One kind enjoys three watery estates:
off Tanzania, South Africa and Mozambique.
A second species formed, some fifty million

years ago, not long in coelacanth time,
when the movement of tectonic plates
granted access to Indonesian depths.

Coelacanths, strange to modern eyes, bear
the offbeat majesty of all surviving ancients.
But their slow rhythms and special wants

reduce resilience. A port is planned
in Coelacanth Marine Park in Tanzania,
whose inmates, numbering a few hundred,

are the pivot of repair for their species.
See into the deeps with them and they are
your life too. Then what about this port?

Platt, J., *After 400 Million Years, Coelacanth at Risk of Extinction* (4 Mar 2015), bit.ly/1zYq5z2, retrieved 1 Feb 2017.

For the US government's decision to list coelacanths as endangered, *see Proposed Rule to List the Tanzanian DPS of African Coelacanth as Threatened Under the Endangered Species Act,* NOAA, 80 *Federal Register* 11363 (3 Mar 2015).The listing is intended to prevent entities governed by the laws of the United States from contributing to the coelacanth's demise.

For their red listing, *see* International Union for the Conservation of Nature, bit.ly/2k3WYfs, retrieved 2 Feb 2017.

Q IS FOR CRYPTOGRAPHY

When I told a cryptographer over oysters
about these poems one day he gave a swift
response. You must promise to write one
on quantum cryptography! He regaled me
then with the cryptographic needs
of Bob and Alice, whose feats and foibles
fill every quantum cryptographic tale:

Bob and Alice have news they want
to share in secret. Whispering won't work
since they're days away. Cell and Skype
are insecure. They'll have to encrypt.

But Eve may be sniffing the network
inimical and vigilant. How will they secure
the sacred data? Try a one-time pad.
It's a private key. You combine each
character of your text with one in the
key, yielding an unbreakable cipher
if and only if your key is random, you
keep it secret and after using, toss it.

The KGB printed them so small they could
sit in a walnut shell on paper that burned
ashless in a flash. Boris and Alisa had
identical pads and knew which page
next Monday let them encode, decode
then tear and burn.

Now we mostly use
a public key instead, built from two large
numbers, both prime. Since the key is
public we can all encode. To decode you
need the primes. The master of the key
conceals these from others, who remain witless,
since it's so hard to factor the primes from
the key. You'd need more power than the
computers of the world or else immortal time.

Here paranoia seeps in, a sign of health
in cryptographers. You can't prove Eve won't
devise a way to find the primes. Or, ever
skulking, Eve could have eavesdropped
and caught them. Then too, brute force
will have its day. When quantum computers
grow up they'll factor the primes fast.

So how will Bob and Alice keep it secret?

The quantum world offers ethereal one-time
pads. It all starts small. Entangle two particles.
Separate them and they mirror each other.
Change the spin of one and its partner, now
on the other side of the world, matches it
at once, faster far than light can move between
them. Let Bob entangle electrons, then share
them with Alice. Each can measure their lock
step particles and so build up a private key.

Einstein discovered and hated this wedding
of entangled particles, calling it spooky action
at a distance. Not ready to believe, he said
there must be a force that connects them,
something we just don't know. If there were,
Eve could tap it and maybe break the code.

Many tried to show old Albert wrong, and
no force was hidden there. But they never
closed all loopholes. The world awaited final
proof. It came recently from a lab in Holland.
Particles entangle cleanly. No carrier wave
moves between to let them stay in synch.

Alice and Bob rejoice. They can now build
a shared key safe from Eve, a one-time pad
for our times. They entangle particle pairs
then separate them, one to each. They
measure their spin and bit by bit compose
a key. If Eve listens in and measures, she
will give herself away to Alice and Bob,
who another quantum rule protects. As
Heisenberg showed, when you measure
a particle you change it. So Eve will always alter
where she enters and thereby leave her paw print.

The monogamy of entangled particles means
Alice and Bob can even use a device they
buy from Eve to do their sharing yet keep
their secret. The quantum world offers the
randomness they need, and Heisenberg stands
guard over them.

They now only must believe
they have free will, that no one dictates all their
actions and knows their secrets in advance.
But without free will the game is anyway a bore.

Ekert, A. *et al.,* The ultimate physical limits of privacy, *Nature* 507, 443–447 (27 Mar 2014), doi:10.1038/nature13132.

Ekert, A., Quantum cryptography based on Bell's theorem, *Physical Review Letters* 67, 661 (5 Aug 1991), doi.org/10.1103/PhysRevLett.67.661.

Dasgupta, S., *et al.*, *Algorithms* (New York: McGraw Hill Higher Education 2006), 39–42.

Hensen, B., *et al.,* Loophole-free Bell inequality violation using electron spins separated by 1.3 kilometres, *Nature* 526, 682–686 (29 Oct 2015), doi:10.1038/nature15759.

Brooks, M., Trust no one, *New Scientist* (31 Oct 2015), 37.

Ringdown

Two black holes are about
to marry, a billion years ago.

Circling each other near light
speed then inspiraling, the dark
bodies merge and do a three
beat ringdown, radiating away
imperfections from their ideal
coalescent shape by gravity wave.

This wedding song is like running
the back of your hand along piano
keys from lowest A up to middle C
and it releases ten times the light
power of all the stars and galaxies
we see when we look out.

I first ran LIGO in my mind in 1994
in my living room in Santa Fe
when news of its building went out.
I felt it would find the black holes
and gravity waves set loose by
Einstein's pen on paper in 1916.

A noise at the window pulled me
from reverie. The hummingbird
was tapping his sabre beak.

I'd forgotten to fill his feeder and
wondered would the gravity waves
he might make, if his nuptial soaring
turned assymetrical, ever be heard.

Abbott, B.P., *et al.* Observation of Gravitational Waves from a Binary
Black Hole Merger (LIGO Scientific Collaboration and Virgo
Collaboration), *Phys. Rev. Lett.* 116, 061102 (11 Feb 2016), doi:http://
dx.doi.org/10.1103/PhysRevLett.116.061102.

Twilley, N., Gravitational Waves Exist: The Inside Story of How Scientists
Finally Found Them, *The New Yorker* (11 Feb 2016).

The end of time

There's no time out of mind
time's a powerpoint
we flick to tell our story
it's our mistake
to project it universal

Time's always local
slower in the Mariana Trench
than on Everest
slower yet for the cosmonaut
as she nears light speed

At the ultimate level
there's only a shift in things
one against another
hydrogen atoms fusing
in the Sun's hot core

At the end of story
we drop time
death is not lived through
we need no time then
make no mistakes

Jha, A., Our sense of time is our ignorance: Interview with Carlo Rovelli, *New Scientist* (25 June 2016), 44.

Too few to fill the sky

Have you ever looked up and wondered
why the sky is dark at night? It hit me
as a boy when I stared out from my
New York backyard. Consider it
this way and you will share the puzzle:

If the stars are so numerous as
to seem boundless, why is every
spot when we look up not filled
by a star, each of them a sun?
With such radiant coverage why
is the night dimmer than noontide?

This paradox piqued the German
astronomer Olbers in the nineteenth
century and bears his name. But Olbers
was not the first to hold this worry close.

Edmund Halley, immortal for his
comet, posed it earlier: "if the number
of Fixt stars were more than finite
the whole superficies of their
apparent Sphere would be luminous."

Edgar Allan Poe, shortly before he
died of an 'inflamed brain' and
was found in a gutter staring up at
stars, hefted a chunk of the answer:

"the distance of the invisible background
[is] so immense that no ray has been able
to reach us at all." Lord Kelvin argued
much the same half a century on.

The answer we give today to the way
they posed the problem shows our
own view of the Universe. We now
think the size of space is infinite, while
the number of stars is finite. Trillions
of stars are not enough to fill the sky.

And there is also this: like you and me
stars have biographies and lifetimes
and are younger than the Universe.

So some stars' light has come
and gone and the light of others
has yet to reach us, while many
stars are waiting to be born.
What lies ahead for the sky at night?

As the Universe expands and space
grows larger, our organic or mechanical
descendents will see ever fewer stars
till in a far future the sky will be pure
black velvet without a hint of light.

The sequence of pondering the dark sky paradox among those mentioned above, a subset of those who considered the problem: Halley in 1721, Olbers in 1823, Poe in 1848 and Kelvin in 1901.

Harrison, E.R., The Dark Night Sky Riddle: A 'Paradox' that Resisted Solution, *Science* 22, 941–95 (23 Nov 1984), doi:10.1126/science.226.4677.941.

Harrison, E. R., The Dark Night Sky Riddle - Olber's Paradox, *Proceedings of the 139th Symposium of the International Astronomical Union* (1990).

Beyond answering the problem posed by earlier thinkers, we have a new riddle. Big Bang theory introduces a more modern version of the Olbers paradox. When the Universe was still compact, after it had become transparent and light began to shine, it was in every direction as bright as the surface of the Sun. So where has this radiance fled and why is the sky dark at night? The answer is that the expansion of space causes redshift, the light reducing in energy and stretching out to longer wavelengths. That early radiance has been lowered to microwaves, some 1100 times longer in wavelength and well below our visible spectrum. This microwave background radiation is still clearly visible in every direction to our instruments tuned to its frequency.

Never forget red dwarfs

Red dwarfs throughout all space
and time since the origin
of the Universe are still with us.

These slow burners have planets
too. Their Goldilocks zone, neither
too hot nor cold but just right

for life, is close-in since they are
small cool stars. You'll often find
Earth-sized planets orbiting.

On a dwarf's world, look up. You'll
see the reddish sun hang heavy
and close as your terra firma whips

fast round it. Then consider this:
more than three fourths of the stars
in our galaxy are of this dim kind.

Their longevity makes generous
time for life to rise. Now forty-two
radio telescopes in California

are looking for signs. Join me
to await the results and meantime
let's cultivate a fondness for red dwarfs.

Lada, C.J., Stellar Multiplicity and the IMF: Most Stars Are Single, *Astrophysical Journal Letters* 640 (2006), doi:10.1086/503158.

Gale, J., *et al.,* The Potential of Planets Orbiting Red Dwarf Stars to Support Oxygenic Photosynthesis and Complex Life (2015), arXiv:1510.03484.

"New Search for Signals from 20,000 Star Systems Begins," *SETI Institute* (30 Mar 2016), bit.ly/1M5biP1, retrieved 1 Feb 2017.

THE BIGGEST STAR

In a constellation called
The Altar, in the star group
Westerlund 1, lives a red
super giant busily dying.
It has cloaked itself in a
nebula of hydrogen atoms
stripped of their electrons.

This gossamer veil shows
the next act is in the wings,
as W26, three thousand
times the diameter of the Sun
and the largest star
in the known universe,
sheds its outer layers to propose
a supernova to any watchers
from across the galaxies.

The star will enrich its outer layers
through nuclear reactions then
spew magnesium and silicon
good for making planets. How this
happens and how it affects the star's
vital life is still a mystery.

When W26 blows it will eject iron,
good for making blood
and gold, good for filling teeth.

"Biggest Star in the Universe is Dying, Astronomers Say," *Agence France Presse* (16 Oct 2013).

"How the largest star known is tearing itself apart," *Royal Astronomical Society* (16 Oct 2013), bit.ly/2ksz9P9, retrieved 1 Feb 2017.

Wright, N.J., *et el.,* The ionized nebula surrounding the red supergiant W26 in Westerlund 1, *Monthly Notices of the Royal Astronomical Society: Letters,* Vol. 437 no.1 (1 Jan 2014), doi:10.1093/mnrasl/slt127.

COSMONAUTIKA

The crown jewels of Russia were
never owned by the tsar. I saw
them in London's Science Museum,
in the shape of Soviet spacecraft.

Sputnik 1, a golden sphere
of Brancusi élan, four antennas
to stream back the ping,
ping, ping, I heard with all
the world, the sound that said
we're a species for the stars.

Then the chromed surprise
of Sputnik 3, lofted from Baikonour
Cosmodrome, and in each of its details,
the mother of all Daleks.

I didn't expect to be so touched
by craft the cosmonauts rode home
from the hostile realms of space.

How small and flimsy, scorched
and battered the capsule that
Velentina Tereshkova, before
that a textile worker, flew alone,
the first woman in space, in 1963.

How did she find the heart to fly
that fragile vessel and how intimate
to see the ventilation suit she wore
in flight, its left shoulder embroidered
with the dove of peace.

Then there's the letter from
schoolgirl Maria Kartseva, who
volunteers to fly to the moon.
She writes in 1959 that she's ready
with her kit: a warm ski jacket,
felt boots and warm fur hat.

I wanted to reach back in time
and enrol her as a cosmonaut
so she could go with Tereshkova
and soar above we gravity bound.

The exhibition, *Cosmonauts: Birth of the Space Age,* is described on the
Science Museum website here: bit.ly/1P3tXFc, retrieved 1 Feb 2017.

A TIME WILL COME

A time will come when we all
have our favourite exoplanet.

Many of them, gas giants like Jupiter,
come with multiple moons.
Some of these planets pull on me
as I lie and drift toward sleep.

We study exoplanets indirectly
seeing the way they dim the light
as they transit their parent
star. Or else we see how

the planet adds a gravitational
wobble to the parent star's
progress through space and
from these clues infer the rest.

Now our vision's so strong
through our telescopic eyes
we find them in abundance.
This week a seven planet system
heaved up from the dark.

And stop whatever you are
fantasizing or worrying about
to mark this passage with me:
the thousandth exoplanet
by our apish reckoning
has revealed itself to us.

This is a quiet turning point
in history, in our growing up
as a species, one worthier of
celebration, though much
less remarked, than the day
the Dow first passed 10,000.

Most stars, now we can see,
have a family of planets
and so their number is set
to outpace the numeracy
of our intuition. My favourite
so far is Kepler 62e. I like it
because it seems so much like Earth.

As I edit the lines above near
Christmas two years on, we know
another thousand exoplanets
in just two years of looking, and
it's clear the written word, unless
on the Web and often refreshed
will not keep up, and that's exciting.

Hogenblom, M., Exoplanet Study Soars above 1,000, *BBC News* (22 Oct 2013), bbc.in/2jVTFEL, retrieved 1 Feb 2017.

Hecht, J., The Truth About Exoplanets, *Nature* 530, 272–274 (18 Feb 2016), doi:10.1038/530272a.

For up to date counts of exoplanets, now above 2,000 and soaring, *see* the Paris Observatory's Extrasolar Planet Encyclopedia, http://exoplanet.eu/, retrieved 4 Oct 2016.

For simplicity I've mentioned two of the four main ways to find exoplanets. For a thorough account of the science by one of the lead practitioners, *see* Johnson, J.A., *How Do You Find an Exoplanet?* (Princeton: Princeton University Press 2015).

By grace of the solar wind

In our universe are more planets
than all the world's beaches
riversides and coastlines
have grains of sand. Life, though,

you will tell me, is a complex
dish of many ingredients.
There may be planets enough
to satisfy the writers of

the Upanishads, but where
will the stuff of life be sourced?
We know that cosmic dust
in our local solar system

is rich with organic compounds
and suppose the same for
solar systems elsewhere. What
is newly known is this: cosmic

dust can also offer that needed
elixir—water. How can dust
carry this precious cargo
through interplanetary space?

Silica shapes the dust and
bears oxygen within. When it's
caught in the solar wind
hydrogen ions penetrate

and water forms. Cosmic dust
is always raining down on planets
throughout the light years
offering all the ingredients
for life to make a feast.

Brahic, C., Water found in stardust suggests life is universal, *New Scientist*
(25 Jan 2014), bit.ly/2kreqM1, retrieved 1 Feb 2017.

Bradley, J.P., *et al.,* Detection of solar wind-produced water in irradiated
rims on silicate minerals, *Proceedings of the National Academies of Sciences*
111, 1732–1735 (2013), doi:10.1073/pnas.1320115111.

Hallis, L., *et al.,* Evidence for primordial water in Earth's deep mantle,
Science 350, 795–797 (13 Nov 2015), doi:10.1126/science.aac4834.

A MAP OF PECULIAR VELOCITIES

Home is where we lay the mammal
down to sleep and so fall into dreams
and between them what is fathomless.

We may wake to kids and pets with coffee
close to hand and wine laid in for evenings.
Extend the sense of home and it may reach

to block or town, China or the USA,
and for a few embrace the world,
but there's more to know as home.

Galaxies cluster into a cosmic web
of filaments and voids, a universal
rhythm that lacks clear boundaries.

Yet our minds are uneasy without edges.
I need to know where my skin ends and
yours begins before we start a conversation.

So does the Milky Way and its companion
galaxies, our own supercluster within
the greater web, have boundaries clear enough

for us to call it home? When researchers
mapped our local supercluster, they looked to
gravity, the force that huddles things together.

They discounted cosmic expansion and
focused on the peculiar velocity gravity
gives each galaxy. Seen this way the motion

of galaxies in a large region of space around us
is inward, and moving toward a dense region
called the Great Attractor. They mapped

the boundary where the galaxies' peculiar velocity
flows diverge like water at a watershed divide
from those in neighbouring regions. Within

the volume enclosed by this invisible surface lies
our supercluster. They named it, newly limned,
Laniakea, Hawaiian for Immeasurable Heaven.

So home is Laniakea now. And by the way,
as our Sun lies on a remote arm of the Milky Way,
our galaxy lies in Laniakea's outer suburbs.

Tully, R.B. *et al.,* The Laniakea supercluster of galaxies, *Nature* (4 Sept
2014), doi:10.1038/nature13674.

For a wonderful film that lets you visualize Laniakea *see* go.nature.
com/1unfUmD, retrieved 1 Feb 2017.

9 781909 954892